The Evolution:
A Mental Rose Series
A Collection of Poetry

*"For I was hungry and you gave me food,
I was thirsty and you gave me drink,
A stranger and you welcomed me,
Naked and clothed me,
ILL and you cared for me,
In prison and you visited me."*

(Matthew 25:35-36)

AUTHOR:
TRICIA MONK, B.A., M.A., M.S.ED

TriState L.E., LLC Publishing

Tri-State LE., LLC Publishing
Copyright © 2022
Edition 1

New York
Printed in the United States of America

All rights reserved. No part of this publication may be reproduced, stored in a retrieval system, or transmitted, in any form or by any means, electronic, mechanical, photocopying, recording, or otherwise, without the notarized prior permission of author, Tricia Monk.

Library of Congress Catalog
Monk, Tricia
Tri-State LE., LLC Publishing
The Evolution: A Mental Rose Series
A Collection of Poetry
Tricia Monk

English Language- Poetry/Free Verse

ISBN: 979-8-9855563-3-9

Order of Poems by Subject

Title page
Title Information page
Table of Contents page
Dedications
Heartbreak
    PSA
    Dear Black Man.
    Stolen Property
    Scarred
    Breakfast Table
    Intangibles
    My Evergreen Tree
    Mirroring Image
    Domestic Violence
    "Mommy, I'm Hurting"

Stolen Dreams
    Old Rooms
    Robbing and Mobbing
    Swerving

Purity of Heart
    Love to Hate
    The New Him
    Versatile: Two-Faced
    Quickstand
    Prepared and Waiting
    Muses
    #RealTalk

    Fallen Love
Generation Alpha
    Mark
DOCCS
    February 28, 2019
Pro-Black
    Our Golden Black Child
    Sailing Backwards
Restoration
    Heaven Knows
    Passion Ties
    Divine Truth
    Baby Lungs
Motherhood
    Nighwatch
    Texas Heartbeat Act of September 1, 2021
    Cinderella in the Hood
    Asia's Wellbeing
God's Love
    Holy Spirit Encounter
    Steal and Seize
    Siddha: You Guide Me
    The Final Say
    9th grade biology
    Grande Colline National Park
    Divine Affection
Sneak Peek

Dedications

Thank you Lord, the Great Divine, and the Holy Spirit that walks within me everyday. I dedicate this creative work to you, as my guidance, and my number #1 supporter. You let me know who I truly am, and how to walk in your light. This text reflects the transition from then-to-now, Darkness-to-Light, and "Backslider"-to-Anointed. Grateful & Blessed. Thank you.

My favorites in the whole world- "Sea Shells of Asia." Remember that you are God's Chosen Ones: Be wise, be smart, be beautiful, and know that you are powerful, and will accomplish all your dreams. Thank you for unconditional love. Thank you for your patience, and thank you for trusting me with your growth. I love you always.

Family: Thank you for being my support circle. Thank you for unconditional love, and believing in me, always. You motivate me, and serve as my drive to "keep going".

Lastly, thank you to all the triumphs and losses that led me to better. To my past-lovers, and naysayers– Thank you for motivating me to strive for greatness. I hope that one day you will "tap in" and find the happiness, and positivity that lies within your core.

Thank You,

Tricia Monk

Heartbreak
PSA
(Public Service Announcement)

NEVER NEVER NEVER put another motherfucker before yourself.
No, I don't curse, nor do I like to curse, but the underline of these words can only be of a curse.

Never, never, put another motherfucker before yourself.
What does that mean?
>It means you're pretty, and your body is right.
>You fulfill another's needs before your self-worth, before self-pride, before your own fucking needs.
>Yup, putting a motherfucker before yourself.

Call it loyalty.
Call it friendship.
Heck, call it love.
Call it everything it is not.
Don't define it,
For, all I knew is, it is what it is.

The moments, motions, ---real dynamic, repetitive, and dramatic.
Sightless, consciously inactive.
Fuck that motherfucker.

16 years onset at 16.
Half a life.

That motherfucker ain't shit.
Fuck that shit.
I say, what I mean,
He ain't shit.

Dear Black Man.

I'm entitled.
Yup, I said, "I'm entitled."
I'm entitled to reparations
R E P A R A T I O N S
I've been wronged

I don't speak of my ancestors
But, of my sisters and brothers

Years of:
- beatings
- neglect
- mistreatments
- servitude
- belittlement
- Rape

- Prostitution
- Ridicule
Forced into shelters with my babies
Food stamps, a constant need

Hands tied behind our backs
Shackles on our feet
Penguining into the courtroom, cause life took its toil.
Are we blind to suffocation?

The air recks of the pungent smell of slaughter
Broken cycle of miseducation
Tutorial to becoming a misfit.
The mistakes never mattered,
The road unpaved.

You owe us reparations
Stop smooth talking and pay your tab.
Stop making Archibald proud.

L O V E,
A Broken Black Woman

Stolen Property
File the police report.
Call the detectives, cuz there's been a robbery.
Momma told me, "I'll never see it again"

"Getting it back, will never happen"
She was robbed at 33
By a foreign nigga

Grandma says she was never robbed,
She's the gangsta one
Niggas tried to rob her, but she's thick and Cuban-born,
with solid protection.
Options and moves made her not give a fuck; so they
had nothing to rob.
Disappointed and embarrassed, so they fled.

My sister's robbery—a bit consistent. A night petty thief
that takes little by little, the unrecognizable.
Chips at the surface, till you're blindly stripped; fully
unclothed, dismantled, dismembered.
Scene left untraceable
So a return is inevitable.
She's often robbed.
Robbed the most I've known.
Oblivious that she's a victim—- pierced, marked, and
targeted.
Just like mama, robbed by a foreign nigga.

Auntie was robbed and even murdered.
Cold, bloody, gorry.
Long-term robbery,

Disrespectful type, left her feeling slow, belittled, and ill—mentally and spiritually.
A forced-hand robbery.
A in-your-face, daylight violation.
Haitian-born, hunger subsided– so decisions swayed—- slighted, and limited.
An old fool walks around elated at his completed robbery.

Find an escape from trauma
Find salvation— the only redeemer
Robberies are temporary, you'll get back your loss and thensome.

These expressions and observances won't guarantee that you will not be a victim,
one day or another,
once or twice.

If all else fails,
    pick up a pen
    flow within your purpose
    ——holding fast to your emptiness
    avoiding that you too have been robbed.

Scarred

If they see your scars, they'll know exactly where to cut for it to hurt.
So, you conceal the scars in fear of multiplication,
Only impeding healing, from the lack of sunlight to your open wounds.

Help the broken babies,
Little babies,
Help them master their thoughts, and emotions.
    Even those hidden, visible, scars.

Breakfast Table

It started at breakfast
Conversations to outline our day.
Discuss the goals, the highlights and the inevitability of foreseen lows.

But, today was a bit different.
Your eyes reflected a closed conversation.
Closed to me,
Discussed with a third party undisclosed in our home.

The eerie smell of the dew in the morning is only viable in reflections.

Breakfast untouched.
Plans scheduled
You were already out the door.
All words unspoken:
> " I have to tend to the developing man."
> "The child living within my past."
> " I have a meal prepared, already waiting."

Yelling, friction, chaos,--resulting in the inaction of my true feelings.
16 years.
16 years.
16 y e a r s.
Discarded,
Trashed,
Banished,
Stripped, naked of 16 years.

Internal ridicule of shame.
Sit,
Eat,
Let's talk.
Mind concluded.
Bags packed.
Smiles resonated on your disguise.

How?

How does one walk away from a solid home?
A home build of precision.
Taking your chances on EMPTY
You kiss my forehead, saying "I love you."
How?
When? –16 years ago?

Breakfast never tasted so bitter,
    Till this day.

I'll be damned to take a seat in the morning dew and be cuddled out of my reality.
So, I changed my routine.
    Rid of the toast,
    Rid of the eggs.
Fuck my day!
    Let the divine guide my steps, for I'm officially broken.
    Shattered to pieces
    Left here at the breakfast table to reflect.

Intangibles

Hold on fast to your intangible,
      For thieves are lurking to encapsulate it, and
seize it away.
For the intangible sways in space and time.
Vulnerability to the open realm.

False ownership,
Borrowed for a moment,
Released back into the inner being —
alone
neglected
and unidentified.

Yup, he stole and manipulated my heart.
I continue to lend it out, in hopes of a multiplied return;
      zero, ontop of zero, ontop of zero.

Does man know the true worth of the intangible heart?
Why mistreat what matters the most?
For God uniquely designed and assigned the heart for
fulfillment of the needs of others.
For the intangible heart needs a partner for activation.
Failed attempts leave the heart distressed, rejected, and
waiting.

My heart is beyond vulnerable—
      The key component of my spiritual world.

My Evergreen Tree

I want to utter those words
      "I love you"
I want to look you straight in the eyes, and speak to your heart

Declaring my moment for you.
I want you in the wantest most part of my soul.
To profess my love to you.

Why hold it so close?
I'm restricted from its release.
Will I be barred?
Will I be neglected,
      ridiculed,
      foresaken
      or even worst– ignored.

Take me seriously.
Know I love you.
Your touch activates my love.
Your words caress my passion.
Your energy reignites my wisdom:
      you are love
      my love
      my companion
      my moment of breeze.

All my wants derive from you.
My source of fulfillment.

Let us stand still.
Let us stand firm.
Let us stand unmoved–
 unmoved by the surrounding world.

Just like an Evergreen Tree,
My love for you is everlasting,
 —beauty within the soul
 —mesmerized by your flesh.

The beauty of His grace within us—
 Maximized.
Spiritually married.
Romantically involved;
 Aroused,
 Invaded,
 Persuaded,
 Confirmed.

Your image is imprinted in my mind.
My Evergreen.

So here I say, *"I love you.*

Mirroring Image

A deadbeat dad dies of unknown details.
No one gave a fuck;
Just like he lived his lifeless life.

    RIP Deadbeat.
    Thank you for life.

Domestic Violence

I knew domestic violence
I knew about loving a nigga so bad,
You'll allow him to choke you out on a trailer,
While his baby mother visits the next day.

I knew domestic violence before,
When you thought you were so fly,
Turn your nose up at other ladies,
All experiencing the exact same wave.
Hours before you were getting called "bitch" "hoe"
"slut" and "dumb."

I knew domestic violence
When the niggas mouth would fill up with spit,
Trying to say, "I'm sorry," and "baby I love you."

I knew domestic violence when bruises and bald spots became a badge of honor,
Accompanied by "double digit anniversaries."
—- Never leaving.

Sitting in the salon chair, 4 bundles can't cover these holes.
Got caught with a white woman, black/white woman, old woman, hoodrat, voodoo-doll woman, sized XXL woman, size S woman, Dominican woman, "around the way" chick, throwback-repeat woman, even an outta state woman.
Smiles and laughs for days, at the one who has befriended domestic violence.

I knew domestic violence, until the day I decided to part ways,
Forget our old acquaintance.
Ultimately, I controlled our relationship.
Deciding life over death.
Bondage released in just an instance.

"Mommy, I'm Hurting"

Have you ever fallen in love?
Have you ever experienced heartbreak?
The kind of pain that leaves you physically and mentally distorted.
Ill, not wanting to change space, or pace.
Wondering if you're the sole victim of sorrowful expectations.

> *Do your best,*
> *Dress your best,*
> *Exhibit politeness.*
> *He'll come around,*
> *He'll eventually change.*
> *Silly daughter, I've raised you by myself.*
> *You emulate me,*
> *Idolize me,*
> *But choose not to trust me?*

> *Trust that I've experienced and conquered hurt.*
> *It's only a season; not even a very long one.*

But why Mama?
I loved him dearly.
I let him have all of me to make him whole.
Am I not enough to make a man love me?
To love our children?

To love my intricate feelings and aspirations?
Is he yet not whole?
What does it take to make a man whole?

> *Please love, speak, mommy is listening.*

I no longer have pieces of me to offer.
But, maybe over time I'll settle.
I have no more, for another.
No more materials to build a home;
I gave him all of me,
All my materials,
All my earnings,
All my energy.

I'm calling it quits, in hope of regenerating inner strength and value.
Mommy, will I rebuild me?
How, and where should I start?
I'm empty in all areas.

> *Well my girl, have you worked your last job?*
> *Have you traveled your last voyage?*
> *Have you encountered your last friend?*
> *Have you made your last dollar?*
> *Laughed your last laugh?*
> *Cried your last tear, and kissed your babies as a finale?*

Have you written your life off?
Created your Will, and ready to die?

Embrace this shedding and blossom.
Blossom into your transition, and embark on this new journey.
It is written, just follow the script.
No longer cross their "t's" and dot their "i's".
Be you, flow as you please.
Explore and build to be the best version of yourself.
Connect with God, like never before.
Tap in.
You will never, never let yourself down.
Others will hurt you,
confine yourself.
Identify and seek your expectations.

I love you.
You are Chosen.
Love yourself even more.
Strive to be whole,
For the timing of his growth it's only for God to know.

Stolen Dreams

Old Rooms

I hate this little old room.
From the murkiness of the door's grim greeting,
The hardwood creaks of abandonment; sound by sound,
footstep by footstep, tear by tear, year after year, month
after month, day after day, hour after hour, minute by
minute, to the seconds of visitors.

The bare walls of time. Hollow holidays, shells of
smiles, eye sockets forever diluted.
Plates of scrapes, mini bites, poverty's prized child.
Surrender your thoughts, it will never be.
Compromise to happily live in this little old room, with
pride.

Compromise the aspirations of achievements.
Suspend the thrive for equality, sensibility, and
intelligence.
Broken furniture, rationalized for mental vintage.
Vintage holdings, vintage clothes, subdue invigorate
motives.

Though these durable chains never rusted
away—-America's best investment: We become at peace
in our hearts; acknowledging that we often share despair
from unattained dreams, deferred travels, obstructed

opportunities, and resentment for our neglected kinsmen and women.

Look around this little old room. Wall by wall, square foot by square foot.

Filled with love and pride of our experiences and persistence.
Persistence to reflect back on this little old room, and say, "I once stayed in a little old room, but then I opened a book."

Robbing and Mobbing

I want to rob a nigga,
Rob a nigga, like they have been robbing and mobbing for years.

Get in his whip,
Straight down the Palisades.
Make him elated,
Swallow. Numb.
Make his toes curl.
Moan and groan.
Make his eyes close tight.
Yup, he's obsessed.

Bring him back to the crib, gushy.
Put him to bed,
Commit a robbery.
Take the money, jewels, and the iPhone.

Leave him a note:
"A robbery under surveillance." Yup, I got the footage.
I robbed and mobbed him of his manhood, like he did my son.

> *And if you ask yourself, why has this happened to me? It is because of your many sins that your skirts have been torn off and your body mistreated (Jeremiah 13:22 NIV).*

Swerving

Silent whispers in my ears,
Swerving for me to move maliciously.

I need to grow,
Hoping to one day grow from the traumas within.
They haunt me like the knife of a hungry, scared, scarred thief.

The embattlements of a single parent.
Fists to face, blood out the nose.

Whispers.
Whispers to never move,
To never make a sound,
clinched behind the living room couch.
Yells, scatters.
Hate derived from possessiveness.

Ownership according to paperwork.
Paperwork to make a day's minimum wage.
Wages leaving them hungry for hours, days, and weeks.
Mayo sandwiches, delinquencies at its finest.

So, acknowledge the malicious attempts of those thoughts.
Firmly rooted from underneath.
Underneath the veins of your blood, the temper of your responses,
The frowns of your heart.
Hate.
Hate those that cause pain.
Their purpose is demise.
No one man should hold the key to your sanity, like he does.

Purity of Heart

Love to Hate

You know, I've met hate before.
Yeah, it's very ugly
It's never seen, yet all too familiar
Hate doesn't knock on the door announcing its arrival
Yet, very boldly,
It rests within the larks of the forest.
Seen, yet very unseen
It's slowly paced, discreetly imposed;
Overtime evolvement

I need him back.
I yearn for his return.
In the midst of my silence, the tears begin to flow,
The smooth jazz of S A D E.

I smell hate to this day.
The look of your direct daze, pierced my vision,
Like, ate at my heart, and shattered my fondest memories.

I encountered hate the day my nose became clogged on the drive home from your
S P I T on my face.

Ashamed, yet redeemed, and forgiven.

Missing the illusion of love.

I've met hate before.

The New Him

When I first saw you,
I wanted to make you to be–
The New Him.
You make me anew;
Like a teenage love.

The New Him
Makes me calculate a new beginning
Rethinking my current stance
I want to be wherever he's at

The New Him
Nothing like the old him
Lingering in the scents of my natural moisture
Kisses my love handles
Caresses my fears

The New Him
Has me finding a new me.
Hoping for mental elevation
Consciously aware.

Spiritual Healing
I've found my equal match in—-
——The New Him

Take me as you want
Take me old,
Take me new,
Take me holy,
Take me sinfully.
The New Him handles me all so well.

Versatile: Two-Faced

He has double faces.
It's not always negative to be two-faced

He was two-faced and yet it was so dope;
A thug in the streets,
A lover in the sheets.

Feared amongst the niggas,
A protector of my figure.

Quick to pull the trigger,
Fuss with me never.

Soft spoken with his beautiful Gem,

Fuck Dem.

He has double faces.
It's not always negative to be two-faced

Spending little with others,
Cuddles me, feels on my breast, and compares my touch to that of a mother.
He's a true lover.

His name rings bells,
Niggas tremble cause they see hell.
His eyes only tell me of my sweet smell.
I wish my prophecy can foretell of how he loves me genuinely all too well.

He has double faces.
It's not always negative to be two-faced

Quickstand

They fell in love quickly
But, they express it not.
They fell in love at the moment of "hello."

The heart found its match,
But, the flesh interfered.
They fell in love whenever their eyes met.

He gazed at her underneath his disguise.
She captured the moments, and seized the love.

She fell in love when they had their first date.
Held hands,
Flirted with the brushes of the souls.
An instant divine connection,
dismissing the resonance of the mind.

They've known each other.
They've lived together.
They've cried together.
All in another dimension.

They fell in love,
Centuries ago.
When he entered her realm at the very first "hello, he felt it.

She confirmed it.

They fell in love without ever uttering those syllables.
For the thought of madness would certainly subside.

So, carry on with introductions, and awkwardness.
Society tells us when to love;
But, we fell in love at our very first "hello."

Prepared and Waiting

I'm ready
I'm ready to tell you that you make my heart smile.

I'm ready
I'm ready to gaze into your eyes and see my future.

I'm ready
I'm ready to walk at your side

I'm ready
I'm ready to become one flesh, one soul, one being with you.

I'm ready
I'm ready to arrive at my destiny.

I'm ready
I'm ready to spend my exciting and boring days in your space.

I'm ready
I'm ready to laugh, cry, rejoice, and rationalize with you in my reflection.

Crooked path, turned straight
Divinely selected
I'm prepared for this very moment.

Be prepared, stay prepared, for when destiny calls, you shall follow.
No time to pack
No time to debate,
No time to inform the others.
Secure your space, for it's a brief moment in time.
A brief moment to be fully aligned with your true love.

Muses

Around 05' August taught me
Taught me to have a muse.

So, I kept two.
Split my influences
Divided my inspirations.

Vibrations of love and passion
Give way to fierceness and courage.

My two muses
Enclose me.
Creates and destroys my shield,
At the same time.

My two muses
Reflect my Mars and Venus.
My hello, while longing for a goodbye.

My two muses
Encompass the loudness of silence
The isolation of my illuminated presence

My two muses
Exhibit the fierceness and gentleness of love
Underlying the discreteness of hate and jealousy.

My two muses
Never fail me.
    A idea
    A message
    A lesson
    A story untold

My two muses
    Loyal by default
    Darkness vs. light
    Blindness vs. Sight
    Flesh vs. Spiritual

My two muses
    Never to collide
    Parallel movement
    Keeping me on track

My two muses
    Commitment vs. freewill
    Love vs. lust

My two muses
    Beings; Never to personify

My two muses
    Truth vs. Reality
My two muses make it a third party situation.

#RealTalk

Truth is, *I love you*
Not really,
Truth is, *I still love you.*
Truth is, *all this hurts, like it's the very first day.*

Truth is, *I'm full of faith.*
I believe *we have been resurrected.*
I believe *His Spirit walks with me.*
But, truth is, *His timing frustrates me.*
Truth is, *I'm impatient.*

Truth is, *brokenness sucks*
Broken, mentally and spiritually —- *Healing isn't happening.*
Broken in affairs of my Heart— bleeds daily.

Truth is, I have faith,
He heals all, — as He always has.
 —- Silently, I wonder *will He change his mind?*

Truth is, I feel like maybe I'm not them.
  So, it may never happen for me.
  Insecurity at its finest.

Truth is, I love my thickness, all my curves and swerves,
But, I aspire for equal likeliness in my partner.
Truth is, *I hate to fight.*

I'm a lover
> Very shy
> Easily offended

Truth is, *I want to*
> Hurt him, then heal his wounds.

Truth is, *I want to share my story*
> As long as you don't comment–,
> Or just disguise that you're listening.

Truth is #RealTalk

Fallen Love

A divine love, not perfected,
for time intervened.

Time had its say and dissolved our connection,
In a smitten of time.

My love for every part of your being— accelerated.
As it accelerated, it deflated just as fast.

Time moves so slowly to the eye,
Yet so quickly in eternity.

Our connection– eternal

Steadfast.

Defiant I will not be.
Grateful for the opportunity to encounter divinity's selection.

My silent soulmate,
My divine love-crush.

Kiss me under the stars, then send me home to live out my destiny.

Fallen (adj): **THEOLOGY;** *subject to sin or depravity.*

Generation Alpha

Mark

They use you to:
- Embarrass me
- Abuse me
- Ridicule me
- Endanger me
- Betray me

Your intentions, those were not.

My influential moments
My happy moments
My calls for prayers
My sorrows and downfalls
I even flirt with love.
All my emotions and experiences enveloped in this capsule of time,
Behind these blue walls of deception.

Competition thrives, money is loitered.
Cancer, a commonality.
The distinction between true and false dissipates in the strides.

Captivated, mind manipulated.

I'm a 90's girl, looking for a 90's world.
Real life conversations
- connections
- Intimate moments
- Ambiguity at its finest

Social Media sucks.
Thank you Mark..

DOCCS

February 28, 2019

Clang, Clang, Clang, clang.
Open these fucking doors!
Open these cages and set my soul free!
Release the inner beast
Restricted, Constricted, Deprived, and Reprieve.
Fuck a Repent.

I lost my sanity in that shell of time.
Aspirations went astray,
Love lost in time-- Broken promises, and illusions
Functionally inoperable,

Fucking open these walls!

Reality missed my consciousness, in the midst of chow meals.
Illusions vs. the reality of cellmates.
I'm fucking going crazy in here!
All perceptions distraught with smells of the street,
Oh-- how I'll miss these great visit floors.

Let me out of this cage!
I can no longer be contained,
Wild like a Lion,
I'm ready to eat.

Eat the souls I've held within,
My heart yearns for revenge.

Guard, fuck your keys!
Break it open!
I'll chew these bars, if you give me a chance.

Fuck this prison,
Fuck your sentence,
Fuck the board,
My time is up!

Pro-Black

Our Golden Black Child

Our thoughts lie in your safety.
Universally aligned are our goals for your future.
Redeeming the lives stolen.

Grievances over missed chances,
Proven to be trivial.
Only for you I assign change to generational curses.
Living for Christ's steps,
Defying the odds, and taking risks for hope.
Endless aspirations, despite defeat and trials.
Never be persuaded, live not in the dark.

Beautifully and skillfully created
Learn to tell your own story.
Own youth truth
Admired by all.
Anointed in due season.
Cry when it hurts.
Laugh when life warrants a smile,
For kindness is within you.

Child of the most high.

Highly influential.
A S T A R by design.
In the Word lies your truth and vision.
Look for Grace within Spirit,
———-and G I V E graciously
Discernment will make you reliable.

Seek consistency.

Golden, Golden, Black Child.
U N D E R E S T I M A T E D,
overly misused.

We raise you up,
so your fall, we will always catch.
Remain ours
 never sway.
Whether behind a wall,
or on a street corner,
your plate is fixed, and your bed is made.

Golden Black Child,
you have a H O M E with me.

My apologies for the inevitable hurt of racial piercing
slurs,
rape,
racial injustices,

stagnant steps,
and brutal murders.

OUR BLACK LIVES ALWAYS MATTER TO US - -
Tears for the Golden Black Children who have lost their lives;
weep for only a moment,
We will meet again.

Sailing Backwards

All white everything
Pure bliss
Pure serene happiness
Divinely aligned
Sun Rays from above glistens on the water,
making water diamonds.

Smiles, grins, makeup, perfume
Heels, designer brands,
All white everything

My people are at peace.
Gracefully, hand and hand with loved ones
Photos,
Cheek kisses,
Lipstick,
Glitter.

Ah

All white everything
Evites sent.
Responses overflowed.
A chance to sail only a quarter of God's natural water.
A glimpse, a smitten.
Crushes evolve.

All white everything.
Lining up in the scorching heat, with
—-Sweat pearls forming and stench forming.
Remain calm.
Your moment in line will soon arise.

The waters of my ancestors.
Ancestral courage:
—drugged,
—beaten,
—chained,
— forced migration
— imprisoned contentment.

Waters lined with blood,
drowned amongst the fish
Souls turned mermaids

"Enjoy your boat ride!"

All white everything.
I see the Sea differently.
—-Not the same as you.

Restoration

Heaven Knows

Heaven only knows
    the stories I refuse to tell awake.
    I hear the terrors of my childhood
    The childhood that every waking moment I try to
    escape, diminish.
Heaven keeps my secrets.
    If revealed, who will she be?
    How would she face her children, day-to-day?
    How would respect be granted?
Heaven knows
    The experiences endured,
    The moments sacrificed,
    The risks conquered.
Heaven knows my heart
    Intentions were never destructive,
    Just mincing,
    Immaturity subsiding.
Reverse my vision. Take away my sight.
Take away the possessive moments.

The abuse. The sexual assaults. Release them.
Heaven knows
    I can't carry this dead weight any longer;
    Single motherhood.
    Poverty.
    Broken dreams.
    Sexual exposures.
    Loneliness
    Drug abuse
Heaven knows we suffered.
    Not one escaped; addicts, fiends*, rapists,
    deceivers and idiots-All reside amongst and
    within us.
Heaven knows.
    Keep the secrets
    Redeem us
    Set us free
    Mental bondage
Heaven knows
    —so I floss a bit harder than you
Heaven knows
    I should've been dead
    Resurrected to see what's truly life
    Born to death, and trickery
Heaven knows this can't continue
    Time's up; it's over
    Rally up the angels
Heaven knows when

    it's time to live.
Heaven knows my story, your story, we've all dealt with this shit.
    Immigrants blinded by the white lights, white lines, white lies
The 80's seized the movements.
Heaven knows it was all set to happen:
    Incarcerated mothers and fathers
    Murdered babies
    Slaughtered destinies
    Recreated realities
    Families never allowed to flourish.
The 80's exposed our weaknesses.
    Recked of smells of abuse and theft.
    Your immobility, robbed my future—- Fucked up.
Heaven knows-
    He never tasted his mother's breast milk.
    Contaminated with morphine
    Born high; New York slums
    Name from a Y.O. rapper
    Abandonment at its finest.
Heaven knows I don't know better.
Heaven knows to guide my steps a bit more closely.
Heaven knows,
    So, I don't share my story.

*Fiend: 1. Evil, cruel person or spirit.
     2. An individual who exhibits behavior of addiction: oftentimes it refers to a drug addict.

Passion Ties

Destroy my inner being
Punish my secretions
Drink from my well of fortune
Suckle on the tip of my breast.
Create eruptions of explosions
Vibrations within my soul

Be divisive with individual partial
Waves of me
Rushing further back, hitting my walls

Repeat, Repeat, Repeat
Pop!
Pop!
Pop!
Flow,
Endless Flow.

Mouns of release
Capture my transparent soul,

Merging with yours
We are one.
One being,
One unit,
One identity.
I am of you, as much as you are of me.

Hold me
Capsize me
Forewarn me.
Penetrate, puncture,
Open wounds,
Juices.
Surp it up
Taste solely mine,
Surp her up
Eyes wide shut
I'm in the zone.

Divine Truth

"Hair too coarse"
    Interlocking the natural curls and locks of beauty.
    Unshaken in the strength of your hair.
"Complexion too Dark"
    Complexion of dark chocolate,
    Fruit of my cherished cocoa tree.
    Enclosed closely to me, my dark chocolate prize
    Oh, you're protected within God's natural light.
"Forehead to large"
    Equipped with a mind of clarity.
    A brain encompassed with intelligence to navigate the wilderness of this world.
"Eyes too small"
    Eyes perspiration inevitable, of the labors you will endure; disturbs your vision not.
"Mouth too wide"
    Tongue of manifestation.
    Spoken praises, result in heaven's prompt responses.
"Breast crowns to stern"
    The tender touch and succulent taste of your craftily structured bosom.
    Oh, how I rejoice in my creations.
"Stomach wounds of childbirth— These hips too wide"

      Divinely selected to conquer the wounds of my children's passageway.
      Stretch marks exemplify the strength and redemption of motherhood.
"Butt and legs sized at extra large-"
      Shaped in such a way for you to walk away,
      Gracefully, from any situation not of me.
      Legs to withstand the toils of your labor.

Harvest will be yours, for you've planted the necessary seeds.
Steadfast,instill confidence, for every twist and turn is uniquely designed for you.
You're truly blessed,
Truly intentional ,
Truly ROYAL
      Deserving of all Godly things.
Purposeful and beauty exalts from within

My child, skillful created in the likeness of my image
You've been strategically designed,
According to a great divine purpose.

For these words derive from my spirit:
Boldly spoken.
Zero omitted.
      -So, I stand in my grace,
      -Filled with faith

I defy gravity, and rise up to Christ, for I will not fall.

Baby Lungs

Sickness cripples your tiny lungs.
      The darkness of illness has succumbed to you.
Shots, bandages, machines, attachments, potions of
experiments, gripple the hospital room.

Stern face,
One-on-one,
Mentally strong,
Spiritually elevated,
Emotionally detached.
Rolling through the motions,
      I remain numb.

Your numb to understanding that I'm all you have.
      My mother is foundationally mine-
      I, foundationally yours.
Fathers, only in title.
      A job rarely visited.
      I wonder how they keep count?
Do you count your money, if not in your possession?
      Like a forgotten investment, one day to mature.
      Make your presence known.

Routine sleep amissed.
    Vital signs, ticks, tocks, and "excuse me(s)" .

Holding your miniature body in my arms.
Clouding your sight within my protection.
Cuddling you to wellness.

Mind seclusion-
    I'm bothered by his carelessness,
    Rejoicing at the strength of prayer.
Looking onward to your recovery.
    Breath in, breath out,
    You matter, always.
This darkness of sickness has built a residence
generationally in our home.
    Expelled-
    Detained-
    Exalted.

Take your scientific potions,
Listen to the doctors.
You're divinely blessed.

This darkness turns to light, right before my eyes.

WELCOME HOME TAY-TAY!

Motherhood

Nightwatch

The embrace of motherhood compares to none,
The late night kisses, aligned with keeping nightwatch over what the angels guard,
Encompassed with the shadows of the world, darkness prevails,
Silent loud whispers in the night have no impact on his Grace and glory.

Mama and our Heavenly Father keep nightwatch.

Texas Heartbeat Act of September 1, 2021

So profoundly heartbroken that I don't have the words to say.
Offend you not.

A tale of my remorse, and immense gratitude.
Where would hoodrats, wives, students, single mothers, teenagers, hoes, victims, girlfriends be without the choice?

Not defending an option

A double edge sword, relying solely on one's decision
making capability, overall maturity.
You literally have to be a realist, and fortune teller at the
same time.

How would I know to either throw away my divine
marriage or give birth to another's love child of God?

A cycle of confusion.
A medical decision that no one should have to make.
Abortion– the sweet delicacy of sin.

Cinderella in the Hood

The clock strikes 3am
      New York Spotlights
      New York Flash

The clock strikes 3am
I'm ready to go.
      Glitter–
      Shine–
      Heels–
      All dispersed.

Washing baby bottles,
Reinstating displaced blankets,
Single parenthood emerges at 3am.

Asia's Wellbeing

Overtime I've learned how to heal your lungs,
    For illness aims to conquer,
    Illness aims to be primary,
    Disregards the Lord above.

Lord is the Almighty
    The Prince of Peace
    The Great Divine
    A Mighty Healer.

Therefore, illness I no longer fear.
Illness must flee.
This uncompromising peace lets me control sickness.
Illness has no territory to take—
    My Spirit and angels are steadfast.

So, yes you still get colds.
You experience the sniffles.
You take breathing treatments,
    but I consider your lungs healed.
I declared and decreed:
My declaration, granted.

So, enjoy your childhood,

Play with exaltation.
For the almighty protects all of you—, even those little growing lungs.

God's Love

Holy Spirit Encounter

Speak His language
For I praise His name.

Thank you for choosing me.
Picking me from the rest.

Thank you for always providing the necessary provisions.
I lack for nothing.

Thank you for vision
Thank you for letting me know I've always been enough.
You've validated me.

You, with all your stature whispered that I am enough.
Made me stand on my own two feet.
Elated, respected, intended.
I feel whole like never before.

My heart trembles with joy from the thought of you.

In a moments time, I was restored-, whole.
Instantly gratified only by you.

Praising your name,
Walking in your light.
Eternal light of peace, gracefully accepted.
Privileged, yet unworthy.
Sealed with a Word.

Constant communication,
Reveal to none, till my time has arrived.

Gifts of appreciation,
    I honor you,
    I sing to you,
    I dance for you,
    I rejoice in you,
    And pray to your holy name.
Craving for your presence.
    to hear your voice,
        Hallucination not.

Confirmations solid,
Compared to none.

Speaking your language,

>   strengthens our bond,
>   Solidifies our time, as well spent.

You join my praises,
make song requests,
set daily goals;
spiritually intertwined.
Belonging to your realm;
I'll never sway.
In Jesus' name, I want to occupy this space for eternity.

Sharing the good news of your grace, cause many shy away.
You are peace, love, and abundance.
So, I sit in silence till it's time to meet Him.
Speak to my heart.
"All will be well and new," you whisper in my ear.
It's all love to the Most High.

Steal and Seize

Steal and seize the moment
Dominate the opponent.
They act like they ain't watching

Steal and seize the moment
Conquer the water
Watch the boat floating not.
Your territory, their prize
Your sanity, their guide.
Steal and seize what's rightfully yours.
Never worry about their offense.

Run, hurry.
Steal and seize the moment.
God is waiting for your purpose.
Live in it,
Walk by it,
Dance in its praise,
Own your happiness, it was yours from the start.

Steal and seize
Steal and seize
What's yours is yours.
Have no doubts,
Look in the thicket.

Steal it back.
Seize the moment.
Let no man steal and seize your joy,
Your love,
Your peace.

Seal and See.

Siddha: You Guide Me

You are Jehovah Siddha.
You are perfect in my eyes,
You are perfect to all.
You connect beyond measure.
You carry our troubles
You listen and hear my praises, worship, and worries.

My partner, without judgment, without shame.
I open up to you.
You speak to my heart and Spirit.
You tell me I'm enough.
You show me that I matter.

You matter,
You're a gentle gift,
A prized possession

I cherish your presence.
I cherish your Word.

You are perfect.
You see me as enough
You see me as perfect in your view.
For you, I'm gracious and humble.

I seek you and honor you.
Praising your name is my permanent task.
In the name of Jesus Christ!

The Final Say

He has the final say.
Within the calmness of time, you've spoken clearly defined Words.
Hesitant you are not.

Having the final say,
You distinctively say my next steps.
Disobeying them, I will never.
For all I know, my promise lies within.

I'm greater in your presence.
I'm recovered and redeemed.
I would have never imagined,
    The depth of your insight and impact,

With you, I'm forever changed.
9th grade Biology

God, your Word dissects us.
Peels back our being,
Our hidden place,
Under the multiple layers of our life experiences.

Holding a mirror up to our face
Front-by-Front,
Side-by-Side,
Back-to-Back,
A full reflection.

You dissect our core.
Unmask our truth:
The extent of our love,
The intentions of our givings,
The abyss of our pride,
The secrets of our internal hate
The drive of our passions.

Your Word;
Peels back the layers,
Uncloths me.

I remain bare.

Bare.
Bare,
Ready to serve and to heal.

How else can you heal my broken pieces?
First, I must humble myself and present them to you, in my full strength.
      An empty vessel, within a whole vessel.
A conduit, ready to serve its role as a median, for broken fragments;
      Of various sizes, dynamics, and strength.

So, I seek wholeness within your Word.
In you, I dissect others, while reflecting on me.
In our connection: I listen closely.
You direct my steps.
Dissect me,
Extract the ills my flesh penetrated into my spirit.
Dissect my secret place,
      For when I return, wholeness in your full grace will reign.

Thank you for dissecting me, Lord.
For I know restoration follows.

Grande Colline National Park

A tree falls in the jungle,
No one hears,
But, the tree still falls.

Still
The fruit of the tree,
The precious wood,
All down
Without a sound.

Who redeems the tree?
Who saves the remains of the tree?
      An "intruder," "invader," "arborists" or a "savior"?

I am that fallen tree
Without notice,
Without caution.

The Almighty saves.
For He heard and saw my fall.
He wants to do something new.

Perhaps grow my tree elsewhere.
Perhaps have me produce new fruit.

The fall -unintentional
The redeemer, redeemed.
Saved my mind,
Saved my soul.
In the crowded jungle I stood.
Yet, my fall, isolated in the shadows,
Hidden amidst the crowd:
My fall appeared not.

My Spirit tells me to allow someone to console me,
But, like a Evergreen living tree, one of my seeds,
    branches,
        will metamorphosis and reconstruct;

Reform and become new.
    New grace,
    New wonders,
    New blessings,
    New strength,
    New jungles,
    New aspirations.

So, refrain from sympathizing with that fallen tree.
For it was only a trip,
No indication of finality,
Perhaps, only indication of a rebirth, foretold.

… It is written…

Divine Affection

Dear God,

    I long to see you. To thank you, and to embrace you. Can you please send me a hug from heaven?

Love your admirer,

Tricia Monk

Sneak Peek

Niggas do bids for the loyalty of their niggas,
The same niggas who dont fuck wit ya when a nigga gets sentenced.
Broken friendships at its finest.

No breaks,
No commas,
Straight up 87'
Fuck it,
Catch a case
They real fly out here.
Broken mentalities, for broken realities.

NY, Never a dull moment,

Wildin' Out,
No pause to think of the broken mother fixing up a hot plate.

Gather the spoons,
Cook the crack,
Cause upbringings solidified your doom was cooked.

Burn in the iron cages,
Not Auschwitz,
Cells of AuthurKill.
Kills the blood that runs through your veins.
Stale.
Got you thinking of a broken system.

Doomed to fail since your first jux.
Run, call a few hoes,
Do a few infested ones,
Then expect to be called a real one.

Real, a broken perception.
Leaving you- locked up, and broke,
Looking for an exit.
Straight up 87'

Book Summary
The Evolution: A Mental Rose Series
A Collection of Poetry

Background: When living a life of trauma, with no biological family, and surrounded by fake friends, you quickly rely on God, love, and your girlfriend for survival. Your girlfriend-turned wife, in turn, relies on God, love, and poetry to see life through. Here, you get to hear the stories, humanize the outcasts of society, take part in life-long friendships, and engage in supernatural divinely guided love that only a small group of urban wives and husbands conceptualize.

The Evolution: This collection of poetry that intertwines the evolution of life from trauma, to tapping into the Great Divine for ultimate guidance. The experiences, feelings, and challenges of women, supporting their husbands through life and love, all seeking alignment to the Great Divine.

www.ingramcontent.com/pod-product-compliance
Lightning Source LLC
Chambersburg PA
CBHW040732060526
44119CB00078B/288